I0468106

Crafting Your Brand

Simple Strategies for Cultivating a Successful
Creative Career

Matt Tommey

Crafting Your Brand
Simple Strategies for Cultivating a Successful Creative Career

Copyright © 2013 Matt Tommey. Revised 2021. All rights reserved.

www.MattTommeyMentoring.com

This book or parts thereof may not be reproduced in any form, stored in a retrieval system, or transmitted in any form by any means—electronic, mechanical, photocopy, recording, or otherwise—without prior written permission of the author, except as provided by United States copyright law.

ISBN-13: 978-1482390643

Table of Contents

What People Are Saying

This book provides easy-to-follow guidelines for artists that feel stuck. Matt breaks down the basics in a straightforward way and serves it up with a light touch of humor. So you can stop moping now! Buy this book. Read it. And start making changes, one simple step at a time. If your heart is really in it, you will see positive change.

Wendy H. Outland (aka "WHO")
Consultant to Visual Artists & Arts Organizations
www.whoknowsart.biz

This book is packed with must-have information for every artist looking to turn their artistic passion into a successful art career. I wish that a comprehensive guide like this had existed when I entered the art market twenty years ago.

Philip DeAngelo
Philip Deangelo Art, Asheville, NC
www.philipdeangeloart.com

Good stuff here! Important information for growing your business in a concise format. Loved the activities and exercises to 'make it real' for each person reading this!

Sherry Masters
Art Connections, Asheville, NC
www.arttoursasheville.com

When I was first sent Matt Tommey's book, Unlocking the Heart of the Artist, I thought the book was for artists, and I did not see myself as one. After reading the book, I realized that we are all artists in the sense that we are created to create. Not only will this book unlock creativity within you as you connect to your Creator, you will find yourself mentored and discipled in deep, rich, profound, and yet practical truths. I love this book! You will too.

Robert Ricciardelli
Founder - Converging Zone Network
www.convergingzone.com

Matt Tommey's easy and approachable style of writing shares sound business principles with artists who want to grow their businesses. He shares step-by-step methods that any creative entrepreneur can easily use to increase their exposure and sales, while still loving what they do every day in the studio.

Carolyn Edlund
Executive Director - The Art Business Institute
Art Marketing Consultant
Founder, www.ArtsyShark.com

Matt Tommey's 'Crafting Your Brand', is the kind of book I wish all artists would pick up and use. Not just read, but actually use. Artists are small businesses and Matt sees the necessity of all artists to act like entrepreneurs in order to succeed. The journal exercises and activities along with the comprehensive practical marketing and business knowledge makes this book invaluable to anyone trying to make his/her living in the creative field.

Gwynne Rukenbrod
Craft Curator and Consultant

Whether you're a seasoned artist growing your brand or a hobbyist hopeful, there's an excellent chance that the tip you're looking for is inside this book. Start reading! As a creative person who works with other creatives everyday, I have observed that the distance between success and failure is often painfully small, and yet unfortunately, talented creative people are the ones who struggle the most figuring it out.

It could be time to learn tricks of the trade from a successful artist who has navigated a creative life and mastered his niche over many years -- without bowing to the status quo!

The author brilliantly addresses topics such as 'selling out' versus doing worthwhile business, and many other beauties like 'recognizing and avoiding time suckers'. It's a quick, often lighthearted read especially for aspiring artists, filled with valuable lessons.

Rick Hubbell - "The Slingshot Guy"
Author - Giants in the Marketplace, Davids in the Pew
www.TribeofGiant Slayers.com

As someone who has worked as a promoter and advocate for professional craftspeople for fifteen years, I highly recommend Matt Tommey's, 'Crafting Your Brand.' It is a wonderful guidebook for craftspeople interested in carrying their business to the next level while staying true to their art and creativity. Whether you are a new artist or someone who has been in the field for years, 'Crafting Your Brand' offers practical advice, tools and inspiration to help you focus on the creative road to success.

April Nance

Public Relations Manager - Southern Highland Craft Guild

Former Gallery Manager & Buyer

Introduction

I'm so happy to be finally writing this book after so many years of teaching and sharing these ideas with clients and colleagues alike. So many of the ideas that are in here are not my own, but rather the result of countless lessons I've learned over the years from great teachers, mentors and crazy difficult situations I had to walk through. Luckily, I've come out on the other side with a bag full of tips and tricks to share with you!

My hope is that this book will not be just a simple read for you, but that it will be a guidebook through a process that you are committed to begin – a transformational journey into the life you were made to live as a creative person.

So enjoy this book! Do the hard work and watch for the incredible results as you craft your brand and cultivate the creative career (and life) you've always wanted.

Matt Tommey

Chapter 1

Embracing Abundance: Co-Creating Your Reality

Nobody becomes an artist just to worry about paying the bills. Nobody becomes an artist just to have something to do or to have a job. We become artists because we simply are not happy unless we are doing the very thing we are created to do. We become artists because there is this thing inside of us that will not quit burning until we give it expression. We become artists because we can't do anything else authentically.

For many of us that journey of self-discovery has taken a lifetime. We've all worked jobs we hated, just for the money, in order to get to do what we loved at night and on the weekends, dreaming one day that this could be our real job. We've all sacrificed more than many will ever know in order to somehow get that burning in our creative bones out into a place of expression.

Sometimes I wish that I could've just "POOF" gotten it when I was in college and started out on the creative road to success, but my journey, probably like many of yours, has been a long, windy, scary and exhilarating road that brings me to where I am today. And it's that journey that we all have in common. Each is so very different, and yet, each exactly the same. It's our stories that bind us together.

So, it seems we should have this idyllic experience of life, love and creativity but for many artists – maybe even you – that's far from reality. Too often our story becomes one of trying to make ends meet, sacrificing creativity for profits, making things that sell instead of making things that inspire us. Our creative life can look like a package of too little sleep, growing frustration and an overwhelming feeling of 'is this really worth it?" I wrote this book to tell you that it is worth it. You're worth it. I also wrote this book because I have a passion to encourage you on your creative journey and to urge you to move from just surviving into thriving.

Understanding the unique identity that makes us each an artist is not as easy as simply grabbing a paintbrush and putting color to canvas. For thousands of years, humanity has struggled with what it means to be an artist, even to be creative. The Greeks and Romans even thought creativity was the result of channeling daemons or a disembodied spirit they called a "genius" who would live with, speak to, inspire and create through the individual. Then the Renaissance came along and the focus shifted to the artist being the genius and humanity being the center of creativity, leaving little room for the divine. Even today, the questions remain - is creativity simply some random act of chance, the result of tenacity and hard work, an encounter with divine providence or a culmination of all of the above?

In my humble opinion, our creative sensibilities are not simply the result of well-executed skills or practice made perfect, but rather collaboration between a divinely invested gift, the Giver of that gift and the hard work of artists who steward well the gift entrusted to them. It's on that foundation that everything else in this course rests.

You see, we can't do it all ourselves. We're not wired that way. We can't just make it happen and in fact we don't have what it takes to be all that we desire. That smacks in the face of our good old American work ethic but it's true. However, when we take what we have been given, mix it with hard work and thankfully offer it back to the Giver and humanity as a gift with a heart of joyful expectation, we will always find we have more than enough – fulfillment, creative inspiration and yes, financial provision. Otherwise we end up in the typical starving artist scenario which is based in fear, scarcity and control – working more, getting less, never thinking our work is good enough and always existing in a place of lack and frustration.

As you start this journey, I want to help you do the same thing a GPS does when you are driving in the wrong direction – recalculate. This journey is also about moving from a place of just letting things happen to actually cultivating a successful creative life.

I use the word cultivating purposefully because to cultivate implies action:

- To improve, prepare (land), as by plowing or fertilizing, for raising crops; till.
- To loosen or dig soil around (growing plants).
- To grow or tend (a plant or crop).
- To promote the growth of (a biological culture).
- To nurture; foster
- To form and refine, as by education.

When you cultivate you've got to break up some old crusty dirt clods, loosen up hard spots, water, fertilize and nurture in order to get the results that you want.

As you reflect on your own life and creativity, what are some of the things that need to be broken up, loosened and gotten rid of? For me, three that I constantly have to keep under control are the "I Know" based limiting beliefs and unhealthy relationships.

"I Know" Based Beliefs

You are a result of all the decisions you have made over your lifetime. That may be hard to swallow but it's true. In addition, those decisions and life experiences form a filter through which you see, feel, experience and interpret everyday life. If you're not experiencing the results you want in your life right now then you've got to make a change – not just a change of actions but a change of thought. Instead of always saying "I know that." or "I've heard that before." why not take the approach of "Wow, that's really good! I think I'll try that!" Unless you try something different, you're going to continue to experience the same results you've been experiencing. Be intentional about removing the "I know" filter from your thoughts and be open to new ideas, concepts and methodologies that have the potential to change your life.

Unhealthy Relationships

By this time in your life, you probably realize you are the product of the people you spend the most time around. As kids, we really don't have a lot of choice who those people might have been – parents, siblings, etc. – and believe me, those relationships have made a definite imprint on who you are. However, now that you're an adult, you can choose who you want to be around. Are you around people who encourage you, your creativity and your dreams? Or, are you surrounded by energy-suckers and dream-killers who constantly tear down all the dreams you desire to see built? You can't complain about the things you allow. A big part of learning to thrive as a healthy creative person is being around people who encourage you to be the best "you" possible, people who pour fuel on your creative fire, people who make you feel alive, joyful and full of life. Believe me, anything less is dragging you away from the life you were created to live.

Limiting Beliefs

You're not only a result of the decisions you have made over your lifetime and the people you spend time with, you are also a result of all the beliefs that you've held over your life. For many people, a lot of those beliefs have been based in fear, about things that happened to you or others, or even negative things others have said to or about you over the years. Again, this forms a filter by which you experience life and this filter, if left to its own devices becomes a lid that keeps you from growing, thriving and becoming all you were created to be. If you want to experience all the good things you were designed to experience in this life and accomplish all the dreams that live inside your heart, then you've got to dismantle the fear-based beliefs that are pushing you off track.

Most of us grew up with some pretty warped ideas about being creative or even thinking about being an artist. These ideas come to us masquerading as wisdom from well-meaning family and friends, when in reality, most of them are based in fear from past negative experiences. They can sound like:

- I've got to do it all myself.
- I'm never going to have enough – I should just get used to it.
- I need to get a real job and do my art on the side.
- I should charge less for my work if I want to sell more.

Instead, I want you to begin the process of recalculating yourself to the notions that:

- You have a sacred gift called creativity.
- Your responsibility is to use and grow that gift, in whatever flavor it has come to you.
- You, your work and your purpose in this life are valuable – even essential to helping the world experience beauty and abundance.
- As you pursue your sacred responsibility with a joyful, thankful expectation, the universal source of all abundance will back you up and bring you everything you need and desire.
- You have been entrusted with the power to co-create your reality with God - the universal source of all abundance who gave you the gift.
- Your mind and heart are like an incubator. Whatever the greatest vision is that you see and believe in your heart is the one that will manifest in your life. As the ancient Proverb says, "As a man thinks in his heart, so is he."
- You must take ownership for whatever is in your life now and begin to set your intention and belief toward what you want to see manifest in the future.

Again, the reason I refer to this course as cultivating a successful creative career is because it just doesn't happen overnight. It is a process. For something to be cultivated there has to be clear vision and belief for what it is that you want to see grow in your life. Then, just like a farmer, you must plant a seed (your dreams) into good soil (your heart and mind). Once the seed is planted then there is the work of caring for the seed in the soil in order to finally reap the harvest. At any time during this process, the harvest can be cut short. You must be diligent to guard it so growth can happen.

The process we are beginning today is that same process of cultivation. We are going to develop and clarify a vision, learn how and where to plant seeds, learn to water and care for the seeds and then joyfully expect the harvest. Otherwise, everything you're going to learn in this book will be like pouring water into a bucket with a hole in the bottom. It doesn't matter how hard you work, or how much water you put in it, eventually you're going to keep on coming up empty.

Journaling Exercise:

Take a moment in your own journal to uncover your beliefs about your own creative gift. What do you really believe? Write it down. Circle the ones that are in line with what you want to see more of in your life. For the ones that are negative or fear-based, strike through them and write a positive belief that changes your mindset.

Now take a moment to dream a little bit. What is it that you really want? What's your desired outcome? If money was no object and you knew you couldn't fail, what would your life look like?

Begin to daily meditate on this new dream every day using your newly crafted vision for your life, career and creativity. Let this new belief system take root like a newly planted tree and begin producing the fruit of abundance in your life!

Chapter 2

Who Am I? Determining Who You Are and What You Have to Offer

I can remember the first time I felt that sinking feeling in the pit of my stomach. You know the feeling. It's that feeling you got when you finally realized that not everyone loved your art as much as you do. Oh the horror of it all! Or even worse, the time when I realized that I was not the only artist out there trying to make a living from my creativity. If I had to guess, I'm betting that I'm not alone. The nature of artists is that we tend to think our idea is the best, brightest, most creative and one that's the most worthy of attention, accolade and of course purchase. However, it's not quite that simple.

The fact is, as a creative person who wants to make a living from your creativity, you are both an artist and an entrepreneur; and you have to think like both. It just comes with the territory if you want to be successful. Otherwise you get to play the part of the starving artist who didn't "sell out" to the business end of things. I think you can do both – be extremely creative and true to your artistic passions while making a good living doing it.

Part of that dance between creativity and business is determining with some level of clarity who you are, what you're doing and why others should want to buy your art before another's. Otherwise, you stand the chance of experiencing what many talented artists face every day – having great work that few know about or are willing to purchase. This leads to major anxiety and frustration on the part of the artist, and as for potential buyers, you are out of sight, out of mind. That's why I believe targeted differentiation is the name of the game. Targeted differentiation is simply making yourself unique in the marketplace for people who desire what you can provide.

Unique Selling Proposition

Differentiating yourself within the marketplace is core to what this course is all about and it starts with something commonly referred to as your Unique Selling Proposition (USP)[1]. You may have never heard that term before, but essentially it means identifying what it is that sets you apart from everyone else in the marketplace. You see, you don't have to be the best at everything or even compete that hard with other artists to be very successful. Rather, you have to be the best at something no one else is doing and then find the people who want what you have. Create and control the niche as the expert.

---

[1] https://en.wikipedia.org/wiki/Unique_selling_proposition

When beginning to develop your own USP as an artist, think in terms of:

- What makes your business stand out from the crowd?
- Why should someone buy from you in particular?
- What differentiates you from other artists who are doing the same type of art?
- How are you doing business?

Artist Statement

Once you have clarified what it is that makes you and your artwork unique and special in the marketplace, it is time to put that into a synthesized statement that you can easily communicate throughout as many different media outlets as possible. That statement also becomes the basis for what is known as an Artist Statement.

As you learn to communicate your USP, I want to encourage you to think in terms of being able to verbalize it in 3-second, 30-second and 3-minute sound bites. Your 3-second is your short answer to "So what do you do for a living?" Keep it extremely brief, but tell them about your art. Then when people ask you, "Oh wow – tell me more." you can back it up with a little more depth. Have a few key phrases that get right to the point of what your art is about. If they continue talking to you with something like "That's really interesting…" then you can go into a little more depth with your 3-minute presentation. This allows you to feel out a potential client by giving them targeted information about who you are and what you do without overwhelming them with details right up front. It also enables you to see if they are really interested before spending a lot of time with them in a sales or potential sales opportunity.

Think of your artist statement as a window into your world. What makes you tick as an artist? Why do you do the things you do in the way you do them? What are you trying to communicate through your creative process, choice of materials and end result? What inspired you to get started? What continues to inspire you to create? Remember, your artist statement is a narrative journey about you and your work. It's not a bunch of bulleted resume points. Tell the story of you and your work. That is what sells. Clients, especially collectors and galleries aren't interested in just great products, they want to buy the story. They want to be a part of the story and feel a connection with you, the artist.

Now, some details - I'd recommend your artist statement be no more than a paragraph or two at most. Use easy to read language that will inspire the reader, not confuse or overwhelm them with flowery language, minute details or complicated shop talk. If you are printing out your artist statement, make sure to have your name and contact information on there, along with a few tasteful images of you working in the studio and of your most recent work.

Journaling Exercise

Take a moment right now in your own journal to begin formulating your USP and/or Artist Statement.

Pricing Your Work

I'm not going to take a lot of time to deal with the topic of pricing your work but it has a lot to do with determining who you are as an artist. Why? Because you have to be realistic about where you are in your career, the market you are in and who your potential clients are in order to successfully price your work. If you don't price your work correctly, you'll either undersell your work or end up not selling much of anything. If you want to make a living as an artist, you have to make a profit. I'd encourage you to get rid of the typical artistic entitlement mentality of living off grants, the government or whoever else might offer to provide you a gravy train. Instead, determine your market, understand where you are in your career, target your potential client and price your work where you can make a decent living from it.

A general formula for pricing your work is:

Materials (brushes, canvases, tools, supplies)
+ **Labor** (what you get paid per hour)
+ **Expenses** (heat, air, rent, security, etc)
+ **Additional Markup** (add 20% to all of the above)
= **Wholesale** (your price to galleries)
x 2 = **Retail** (Your price to customers)

While this is a great starting place for pricing, some of the best ways to effectively price your work are to review comparable artist pricing in your region and medium and review your own sales for the past 18 months to see what's selling and what's not. You should always be paying attention, testing price increases and watching how people respond. Pricing your work correctly is key in setting a solid foundation for success. You can't just set it and forget it. It has to be constantly reviewed and tweaked. (Learn more about this inside my book "How to Price Your Art: Pricing with Confidence for Sale and Profit".)

Defining the Field

As you work to clarify your USP, one of things that must be done is to examine the current field of competition. I don't necessarily think the term competition is the best, given our foundation of abundance, but it's mostly correct in describing other artists who are playing in our same sandbox. Take some time to understand who is out there in your niche locally, regionally, nationally and internationally. Find out what is selling and what is not, the trends galleries are seeing, and what price-points are moving. As you begin to understand what is out there in the current marketplace, it will help you further define the niche you want to create within that wider market.

SWOT Analysis

As artistic entrepreneurs who want to grow both creatively and financially, it is important to regularly analyze where you are both from a creative and business perspective. One of the best ways to do that is through what is commonly referred to a SWOT Analysis. SWOT[2] stands for Strengths, Weaknesses, Opportunities and Threats. I'd suggest that on a 90-day basis, you take time to evaluate the total package – your art, business, competition, current market, relationships, etc. – using this tool. Simply take a sheet of paper and make four columns. Then in each column, make a heading using the four items listed above in the SWOT acronym. Now you are ready. Just begin to brainstorm each of these categories. What are the current strengths and weaknesses you recognize? What opportunities are out there in front of you that are yet untapped? Lastly, are there any threats to your success or current/forecasted business model?

This analysis gives you a really succinct way to celebrate and plan at the same time. Celebrate the things that are working, look forward to the opportunities that are ahead and define your course of action. It also lets you understand clearly the potential roadblocks that are set up in your path and gives you an opportunity to consider how to overcome, side-step or avoid them.

---

[2] https://en.wikipedia.org/wiki/SWOT_analysis

Chapter 3

Plan to Succeed - A Simple Yet Powerful Business Planning Model

It is simple yet true: If you don't know where you want to go as a creative entrepreneur then you will spend your whole career responding to other people's emergencies, never really getting to the important things. Planning is simply saying "yes" to the important things, "no" to the unimportant and "get in line" or "you'll have to wait" to the things you don't yet understand.

Prioritizing

We've talked a lot in the last two chapters about clarifying your vision and unique selling proposition and obviously there is a lot that goes into making that vision manifest into reality. A vital part of seeing your vision come into reality is prioritizing your life – planning. By saying *no* to the things that are unimportant or time suckers, you enable yourself to say *yes* to the things that are important.

So what is important, you say? Well, you have been defining that - remember? Your vision for your life and your business, your unique selling proposition, and your artist statement now become the standard – the measuring stick by which everything in your life gets measured. If an opportunity comes along, no matter how good it may seem, unless it directly supports your priorities, you can easily say no. By learning to say no, you begin to craft the life and business that you envisioned. Constantly saying yes to the wrong things only brings confusion. There are tons of seemingly great opportunities out there waiting to suck the life right out of you in the name of charity, friendship, and potential. Say no and you'll get to live the yes.

A great idea for prioritizing your projects is to brainstorm about the areas where you are spending most of your time. Is most of your time being spent in areas that are actually mission-critical for your art, life and business or just other people's priorities you happen to get pulled into. You want to spend most of your time on things that are important to the vision for your life rather than the emergencies that can easily rule an unmanaged schedule.. Once you identify what is going on in your life and business, you can more easily focus on the priorities, saying yes to the right things and no to the time suckers.

Clarity, Creativity, Clockwork & Connection

There are lots of different ways to develop a business plan out there. Just Google "business plan development" and you will get gazillions of pages. Over the years, I've found these four items to be foundational for me and for any solid business plan employed by a creative entrepreneur. I offer these to you simply as signposts you can look toward on your journey of business planning.

- **Clarity:** Know who you are, what you want, where you are going and how you plan on getting there. Don't worry, this is constantly evolving, but it is important that you have the end in sight. Remember, your mind and heart are literally an incubator of your desires. If you can see it, you can have it. What you have now is a result of what you have seen your whole life. To change what you have, you have to change what you see and what you believe about what you see.

- **Creativity:** At the beginning of the day and the end of the day you are an artist. Don't ever lose sight of this. You are not a production center. You are not a marketing department. You are not just doing this to make money. You are an artist because you have been given the Gift of Creativity. Hone your craft, develop your skills, push into the deeper things you see creatively and never lose the spark. If you don't, no matter how much you market and promote, it won't make a difference. At the end of the day, it is about art. Do what you love with excellence, integrity and passion and the money will follow.

- **Clockwork:** Everything in life is about timing and your creative business is no different. I have heard it said that most people overestimate what they can do in one year, but underestimate what they can do in three years. As you plan and set your priorities make sure you are doing it on a timetable that is realistic. One tool you can use is called SMARTi Goals (inspired by the common SMART goals framework.)When making your goals, make sure they are Specific, Measurable, Attainable, Relevant, Timeframe and with an Incentive for achievement. Additionally, make sure that your clock reflects your priorities. You need studio time but you also need marketing time. You need relaxation and family time along with selling and administrative time. Just ensure that your clock reflects your stated priorities.

- **Connection:** More than anything else, I believe in the power of connections. Connection to your inner creative voice, connection to God, the source of all abundance, connection to your work and connection to those around you. Thriving as a creative is, at its core, about continually cultivating these connections. Most importantly, from a business perspective, is what I call "Strategic Partnership Connections." These are relationships with people who are in front of the people you want to be in front of but who don't directly compete with you. They include other artists, gallery owners, suppliers, and the list goes on. We'll talk more about this in chapter six but suffice it to say right now, focus on cultivating these connections. They can become an endless supply of referrals for you for years to come.

Journaling Exercise

Now that you have clearly identified who you are and where you are going, it is important to begin putting a plan together. In your own journal, begin to sketch out your business plan for creating, marketing, selling, strategic partnerships and continuing artistic development.

The Parthenon Marketing Plan

As you craft your business plan, it is also important to consider the importance of your marketing plan. It is so easy to have what I like to call a "silver bullet" mentality when it comes to marketing; thinking that there is one surefire technique that will make all other marketing ideas unneeded, but alas, there is no such thing. When it comes to reality, marketing is more like the movie "The Perfect Storm" than the old TV show, "The Lone Ranger." For marketing to work, it has to all come together to be effective.

When developing your marketing strategy in the context of your overall business plan, I want to encourage you to consider what I call the Parthenon Plan. You know, the Parthenon in

Greece is a huge, ancient building that still stands today because of one simple fact: the multiple pillars that support it. Even over hundreds of years, through countless storms and even treacherous earthquakes, the Parthenon still stands. Your marketing plan can be the same way if you build it correctly. Otherwise, you run the risk of your whole business tumbling when lean times come along or your prize marketing strategy no longer produces.

The first time I heard this multi-pronged approach concept was many years ago when I was working with a business coach in my graphic design business. I think he drew it on a scrap piece of paper and it just took root inside my mind. Come to find out, the overarching philosophy was developed by direct marketing guru, Jay Abraham to describe the effect multiple marketing strategies can have on a company's revenue. However, as I've employed this concept over the years, I've expanded my own understanding of what a true Parthenon Plan could really be for an artist.

Instead of having all your marketing "eggs" in one basket, consider having a minimum of eight to ten pillars that generate leads for you and ultimately support your business. If one or two of them happen to be seasonal, no problem. You still have the others working normally, ensuring regular cashflow into your business. And when it comes to thriving as an artist in your business, regular cashflow is crucial.

Here are some ideas that may work for you:

- Your Website
- Paid Advertising
- Strategic Partnerships
- Referrals
- Art Shows & Fairs
- Invitational Exhibits
- Wholesale Accounts
- Retail Sales
- Social Media
- Email Newsletters
- Teaching Classes
- Speaking Engagements

Remember, the goal is to have at least eight to ten marketing strategies working for you at any one time so that if one of them is not performing at peak, the others can take up the slack. Continue to build your Parthenon Plan with as many tested, successful marketing strategies as you can manage. Ditch the ones that don't work for you and focus on the strategies that produce!

The Parthenon's Foundation

But let's take it one step further. Building a successful art business isn't just about marketing and money. You can be the best marketer in the world, but if your foundation is unstable, you'll be in trouble. That's why I want to you think about your parthenon in these terms:

- **The Roof:** Your Business, Revenue and Brand Reputation
- **The Pillars:** Your Marketing Strategies
- **The Foundation:** 3 Core Principles

There are 3 foundational elements every artist must have in their art business to be successful: an authentic brand that connects with your audience, uniquely masterful art, and a healthy mindset. These three elements are the building blocks for a successful art business and form the basis of a strong Parthenon Plan. Build your business on this foundation and marketing will be the easy part.

Journaling Exercise

Take a moment in your own journal to list your current marketing strategies. What's working and what's not? Now add some fresh ideas to increase the stability of your Parthenon.

Take a moment to find out more about my Online Artist Mentoring Program called "Created to Thrive". From marketing to mindsets, connecting with clients to selling your work and everything it takes to thrive as an artist, you'll get it all as a member of this unique mentoring program.

Find out more at www.MattTommeyMentoring.com

Chapter 4

Say What? Consistently Communicating Your Brand

When it comes down to it, people buy the things they want rather than the things they actually need. Part of our job as creative entrepreneurs is to make sure that what our niche market wants is what we have to offer. The best way to convince them is by telling our story.

Over the years as I've been an artist, author and marketer, I have come to believe one thing passionately – 1 people buy the story. I remember working as a marketing consultant for a nonprofit in Atlanta when one day a patron came to me and said, "Wow, you make this organization look so much bigger than it really is." I replied "Thanks, I'm just telling the story in the best way I know how."

The same has held true with selling fine craft. I'm a basket maker and I've been doing that for about twenty years now off and on. When I finally got serious about pursuing my craft, I did a little research on the field and began referring to myself as a contemporary basketry artist. I also started to notice that the pieces I had always made - functional Appalachian-style baskets - were no longer selling like my other more sculptural, one-of-a-kind pieces. I could make those sculptural pieces in half the time and make twice the money. I enjoyed the process even more and so guess what I started making more of? You guessed it, sculptural, non-functional art baskets.

Another thing I noticed very soon in my basketry career was that people absolutely loved for me to tell them about how I go in the woods, harvest all the vines and bark and then bring them back to my studio for preparation and weaving. It was like the more they connected with the story of me in the woods, the more they were willing to pay for my work. So I came up with a tagline: "Every Basket Begins with a Walk in the Woods." I still get comments on that all the time from customers who just love the imagery and emotion that evokes.

So what does all this have to do with consistent branding? Everything. Branding is simply telling your story in a consistent manner in order to build connection. The better and more often you tell your story, the more recognizable your brand will be. That builds comfort and loyalty among your customers and potential clients, yielding a higher propensity for sales. Bottom line, if customers like you, can relate to you and believe that what you have is something they want, then it's a done deal. Our job? Don't screw it up.

Although brand consistency sounds kind of technical, it is really pretty simple if you keep it simple. From your business cards, brochures, postcards, signs and posters to your booth display, website and Facebook page, everything – yes, everything needs to tell the same story – the story of you. Here are some of my suggestions about consistently communicating your brand:

- **Logo**
  Yes, you need a logo. The more simple and clean the better. It needs to be easily reproducible in color or black and white. It should have strong, simple lines and not be cluttered. Lots of artists use their name, initials, or a studio name. You are creative. Come up with something great and then kick it around with your other artist friends until you get a thumb's up. Once you have it, the logo goes on everything. It is the anchor for your brand.

- **Tagline**
  A tagline is kind of like a 3-second description of your business. It's catchy, memorable and succinctly tells people what it is you do. It should almost always accompany your logo and be on every marketing piece you produce, in print or online.

- **Printed Marketing Materials**
  At the very least, you need a killer business card and postcard. Again, keep it simple and clean but with

high visual impact. Feature your work and let it speak. On your postcard, let one side be a high quality image of your work and on the other let it be your artist statement. Maybe consider a studio shot of you working or another shot of your work. Always include your website, contact information and if possible professional affiliations like guild memberships, awards, etc. If you do a postcard, I'd go for a 4x6, full color both sides. They are super cheap to get printed at many online retailers and well worth every penny. Don't go the cheapo route by printing at home. You're a professional. Invest in yourself.

- **Online Marketing**
  People are looking for you online whether you know it or not. You don't have a choice. You must be online and look good. I will be covering websites, blogging and social media in later chapters but suffice it to say, they are all essential to a solid marketing platform. Even online the same rules apply – consistent branding, consistent imagery, consistent wording on everything. Via website platforms like Weebly, Wix, Squarespace along with social platforms like Facebook and Instagram, it's really easy to have a very professional appearance

online with little technical expertise.

- **Photography**

  Trust me, unless you are a professional photographer or have some level of training, have a pro take photos of your work. I can't tell you how invaluable this will be for you in the short run and long run. Your photography forms the basis of everything you are doing visually with your marketing. If all you have is a bunch of quick shots from your iPhone then it is going to show. There is definitely a place for those quick shots, on social media and blog posts especially. However, when it comes to your professional image that's going out for promo, jurying for shows and talking to galleries, you need professional, consistent photography that really represents the quality of your work.

- **Portfolio**

  It is important that you have your portfolio with you at all, or almost all times. What I mean is, you never know who you're going to meet and you need to be ready. On my iPhone and iPad, I have a gallery of work setup for easy viewing. That way, if I meet someone for the first time and they are interested in what I do, I can say, "Well, would you like to see some of my most recent work?" I've never had anyone refuse. If you don't have a smart phone (for real?) then you can always have a printed portfolio made. Again, don't skimp please. It's representing you, your work and it's a doorway to potential sales.

Journaling Exercise

Now that I've sufficiently overwhelmed you with marketing jargon and stuff to do, let's take a little breather. In your own journal, take inventory of what you currently have in the way of marketing collateral and what you need moving forward. Maybe you have something now but it needs to be reworked to reflect your new brand. Use the space below to start planning your next steps.

Chapter 5

The Balancing Act:
Making Art and Growing Your Business

Back in the early 2000's I stepped out on my own with a Mac computer, some basic marketing materials and a dream of making it as a freelance graphic designer. Until then, I had been working in a creative job within the nonprofit sector but never really considered going out on my own. Things went south where I was working and my wife and I felt like it might be the right time to go for it. So I did.

I can remember those early days - me and my Mac in the sitting room of my master bedroom, working on small business and nonprofit marketing collateral. I'd literally pound the pavement during the day going door-to-door to businesses, asking if they needed any printing, design or web development work. At night, I'd come back and do all the work until late in the night and get back up and do it again.

After a couple of years, like most entrepreneurs that work hard and stay focused, I had business coming in regularly, was making money and was coming to the point where I knew I needed some help. I ended up hiring a business coach who helped me triple my business revenue within three months, which enabled my wife to stay home and be a full-time mom and bookkeeper for the business. I was also able to hire an assistant, expand my design/development team and I literally turned around one day and thought wow, how did this happen? I'm running a business here.

I have to admit that was both a scary and an exciting time for me. On one hand we had lots of business coming in and with that, revenue. That was great. However, what I had to learn to balance was this whole idea of making art and growing my business at the same time. A challenge for most artists! (Michael Gerber describes this concept as working both in the business and on the business inside his book, *The eMyth Revisited*). Truth is, you've got to have both. Great art is the foundation for everything, and your business is the vehicle that takes your art to the marketplace.

As a creative entrepreneur, you have to manage this delicate balance on a daily basis because it is at the core of whether you will be successful or not. Most creatives hate this balance with a vengeance. They want to spend all their time alone in the studio doing what they love. That's great and part of what we've been gifted to do. The other side of that coin is that if an artist doesn't sell that work then nobody's eating. Then in some sort of self-righteous fit, they want to tell us all why they shouldn't have to *sell out* to the capitalistic demands of our society. Hogwash. Again, it's not about embracing one or jettisoning the other, it's about balance – balance for success.

So, let's take this apart. What does it mean for an artist to work inside their business doing all things things it takes to make art vs making their business vehicle run smoothly? If you're anything like most artists, it's the inside the business side of things that you love the most. That would include things like:

- Working in the studio
- Coming up with new creative ideas
- Talking to customers about new commissions
- Filling wholesale orders
- Making deliveries

These are simply the things that most of us as working artists do every day and love. They are probably most of the reason that we even wanted to become an artist in the first place. However, they are only half of the picture.

There's a whole other side to owning your own art business. Whoa! You say, "I don't own my own art business!" But in fact you do. You're not just an artist - you're a business owner whose product happens to be your art. For you to succeed, you have to treat it like such. Otherwise, the creative inspiration you so love will eventually dry up and cause you a lot of frustration because of the intense anxiety of not being able to make a living from being creative. Again, you CAN have both a vibrant creative flow and a successful business plan.

Now that we're on the same page about this, let's talk a little bit about what it means to work on the business side of things. These are the things that you probably know need to get done but are the ones you keep procrastinating about. That would include things like:

- Sending out invoices, billing clients & paying bills
- Applying for shows, fairs and exhibits
- Cleaning your studio space
- Sending & returning emails
- Developing and executing a marketing plan
- Finding new wholesale accounts
- Leveraging social & traditional media
- Working on your website or blog
- Repainting your show booth

Like it or not, if you want to thrive as a professional artist (full-time or not) you have to find a healthy balance between these two sides of your business. The key is to keep the main thing, the main thing – your creativity. That's where the magic comes from, my friend. Otherwise, you can easily get your priorities flipped around and start just making things that you know will sell in order to simply make money. Trust me, that is a recipe for creative death and ultimately business failure. We are not like other folks. We are artists. We've been created to create. Unless we do that authentically, out of a place of true passion, all this business stuff has no value.

Journaling Exercise

Let's stop for a moment and I want you to do an exercise to start orienting your mind to this new balance. In your own journal, make a list of real things you're doing now or need to do. Segment them into things you're doing inside your business to create great art and the things you're doing to make your business operate smoothly and effectively. Then go back and place a number 1-4 by each item. 1 being most important and 4 being least important. Hopefully this will give you a template of where to begin investing your time.

Segmenting Your Schedule

As you endeavor to balance this new way of working, I want to encourage you to think about the concept of purposefully segmenting your time into blocks. Many successful people I know practice this and it really works. Instead of just getting up in the morning and jumping into your day with no plan, backup a moment and start the night before. On Sunday night, take about 30 minutes and look at your whole week. If you're like me, you have everything from studio time and doctors' appointments, to taking your kid to karate lessons and meeting with a gallery owner for lunch. Put all these items on your calendar. (Yes, you need a calendar – preferably one that's on your smartphone so you can access it throughout the day as needed.)

Once you have some of the basics on there – required meetings & appointments, etc. then start looking for blocks of time. For me, I have set aside certain days as "studio time." Other days I know are more administrative. This really helps me because when someone calls and asks for an appointment, I know where to schedule it, and it's not in the middle of my creative time. You have to keep that sacred.

So now you have your big blocks scheduled – creative time, required meeting time, etc. Now, look for some holes where you can schedule your administrative time. These are the times when you can be working "on" the business by sending emails, working on your website, taking work to be photographed or cleaning the studio. I recommend having that as a regularly scheduled part of your week. Again, whatever you schedule, you prioritize as important. That's a big key.

Time Suckers

One little time sucker I've noticed for myself over the years is the topic of email and social media. With smartphones and laptops, it's so easy just to be on those "magic boxes" all day long, no matter what you're doing. By doing so, you're robbing yourself of major creative energy and focus, while also training others that you're available all the time. You're not! Again, prioritize and schedule. One of the best ways to do that is to check your email at the beginning, middle and end of the day. If you can get by with less, do it. Set 20 minutes aside and just bite the bullet, but don't linger. The same goes for social media.

It's important, but all within reason. Set a time to update your status, add new images and interact with people. Then, turn it off.

There will also be things that suck your time that can be better done by someone else with better expertise in a certain area than you. For example, I am a horrible administrator. I forget to pay bills, I miss deadlines and I'm not ever sure how much money is in the bank. So, over the years I've learned to trust my wife in those areas. She's a phenomenal administrator and supports me in my art by helping keep the finances in line. I always say, "I do the weaving and she does the deposits." Don't feel bad about getting help where you need it. You have family and friends who would probably love to help you succeed by volunteering to help you. Or, if needed, simply work some money into your monthly budget to get some help in areas like bookkeeping, photography, website design or other areas where you are not as strong. Again, your focus has to be on staying in the creative zone while managing the total picture.

The Bridge

Lastly, I want to encourage you with a concept that far too many creatives discount. I call it "the bridge." While I most definitely believe we can all thrive as professional artists, I also understand the real financial variables that play into that possibility. You may be one of the lucky ones who just came right out of high school or college, got a degree in art and immediately became a professional artist, making money hand over fist. However, what I find mostly with artists is that their work as a professional artist has been a journey over many years.

Let me dispel a myth. Just because you are a professional artist, doesn't mean that it is your only income. In fact, most artists I know have several streams of income that allow them to be able to pursue their art. For me, I'm an author, a working musician and I still do a little graphic design/marketing consulting work on the side in addition to being a full-time basket maker. I also have an online mentoring program. Does that mean that I'm living a lie? No way! What it means is that I've found a flow that works financially for my family and me. It also means that my income is not solely based on one thing. I like that. It gives me options and freedom. If a basket doesn't sell this week, I know that some books probably will, or maybe I'll be invited to a speaking engagement. It all works together.

Many of you may be reading this book and be working in a full-time job with a dream of becoming a full-time working artist. Let me encourage you. You can do it! But it's probably going to look a little different than you think. It took me several years to move from being solely employed by someone else, with a W-2 and the whole thing, to now being primarily self-employed as a working artist and entrepreneur with a pile of 1099's at the end of the year. I call that process "the bridge." For some it happens really quickly, for others it is a long process. Wherever you are in that process, just understand that it's part of the journey to you becoming who you really want to be. You can't short-circuit it. In fact, it is in those "bridge" times that you have the opportunity to learn valuable skills that can support you when you're out on your own.

The most important thing about crossing the bridge from where you are to where you want to be is regulated cash flow. Begin to develop and increase that in your business, no matter how small you start, and you're well on your way.

Journaling Exercise

As you wrap up this chapter, think about where you are on your "bridge" – are you full-time, part-time, no time? Getting paid? Doing shows? Still working a 40-hour week for someone else? How can you take the next step that will move you closer to your goal? What are the stepping-stones before you? Explore these questions in your own journal.

Chapter 6

Selling To & Selling With:
Understanding Retail, Wholesale & Strategic Partners

Most people think of selling as some difficult process that conjures up images of a sweaty used car salesman, pressure tactics, a few white lies and hope that the buyer will be crazy enough to give you some money. Although we've all experienced that type of transaction, selling doesn't have to be like that. In fact, it can be a beautiful experience for both the seller and the buyer when done right.

I believe selling is less about trying to get people to purchase things they don't need and more about helping people buy what they already want. Let that sink in for a minute because it probably goes against everything you've been taught about selling. The fact is, it is much easier to help people get what they want than it is to convince them to want something you have. That is why understanding your target market is so important. Unless you know who wants your creative product, you can't help them get it. Then you end up frustrated wondering why people won't buy your art when the truth is you're just in front of the wrong people.

For our purposes as artists, sales have two major categories: retail and wholesale. Each one of these categories has a specific audience with its own needs, wants and requirements. It's vitally important to know the difference between the two in order to succeed at either one. Let's compare.

Wholesale Accounts	Retail Customers
Quality	Quality
Salability	Design Aesthetics
Uniqueness	Uniqueness
Profit Margin	Price
Availability of Product Line	Shipping & Return Policy
On-time Order Fulfillment	Connection with Artist
Integrity in Pricing	Convenience

All consumers, whether they are wholesale gallery owners or retail customers, come at purchasing with one question – WIIFM. That's right, the WIIFM. Ready for me to clue you in? WIIFM is a commonly accepted marketing term that refers to the question "What's In It For Me?" Every business has to answer this question effectively for their customers, again whether wholesale or retail, in order to succeed. So how do you answer the WIIFM question?

When we talk about WIIFM we are really talking about the value proposition you are making to your potential clients. That is, why is what you have to offer important to them? It shows you care, that you're thinking of them when you make whatever it is that you make, that you value their relationship with you and your work. Remember, it is more than simply *important* - it is personal. If you can't answer that question effectively, then you are not addressing the WIIFM question.

Also, WIIFM is not about bombarding your potential clients with meaningless, techno-garbled information, it's about making a personal connection with your client. I've always believed that if people know you, like you and trust you they will buy from you. The key is to wrap your product in your personal brand. When people connect with you and your creative story, it connects them emotionally to you and the product. Market research has always shown that people don't buy things they need; they purchase things they want based on an emotional response they are having to the product, salesperson or sales environment. That's why connection is so important.

Wholesale Tips

These are a few of the things I've found over the years that really make a difference when working with wholesale accounts:

- **Make Them Feel Important:** It's so easy to do this by being on time for an appointment, calling them by name, knowing a little history behind their gallery and bringing your artist information packet branded with their logo (you can easily get it off their website). After the relationship is built, address problems quickly that may arise, be responsible, and act with integrity.

- **Develop an Artist Information Packet:** this can be via email or in print. It would include your artist statement, art resume (include shows, exhibitions, collections, education, etc.), a few choice images of your work and any recent press you've received. Again, it just says, "Yes, I'm a serious artist and I want to do business with you."

- **Respect their Jury Process:** Galleries get bombarded with new artists all the time. Inquire professionally about how a gallery likes to receive new artist submissions and follow their guidelines. It lets them know you are a professional.

- **Scout Them Out:** I would recommend, if physically possible that you visit a gallery before putting your work there, unless you know them by reputation or recommendations from other artists. Believe me, they are going to check you out, so do your homework. Talk to other artists who sell their work there, look at the layout, quality of other work and price point to make sure your work will do well there.

- **Maintain Pricing Integrity:** It's so important to make sure your pricing is the same across the galleries you're working with and with your own work. If you're doing wholesale, then protect that relationship by not undercutting your wholesale galleries at your own retail shows. Otherwise, your gallery owners will get a really bad taste in their mouth quickly.

- **Develop a Special Wholesale Product Line:** There are some items I just don't wholesale because over time I've found out they sell better to customers in a retail environment where I'm present. Also, there are some products that I wholesale in gift shops that I wouldn't wholesale to a higher end gallery. Know who you're selling to and tailor your product lines to them. You're not looking for a quick, one time sale with wholesaling. You're looking to build a long-lasting relationship of repeat orders over time.

- **Deliver On Time:** Do I even have to say this? Wholesale accounts are trying to give you money!! Please be on time, courteous and prompt. Under-promise and over-deliver. That's my motto.

- **Stay Connected After the Sale:** From time to time, check in with your galleries to see how things are going. Maybe one item is selling great, but others are stale. You can offer to switch things out, try new products or give them insight into things that are selling well in other galleries. Again, go the extra mile to build the relationship.

- **Promote the Galleries Who Carry Your Work:** You're selling with your wholesale accounts, not just to them. That means you're business partners. Promote them on your website. Do shows that are close to them so you can build repeat business for them after the show is over. Consider doing a trunk show, exhibit or a demo at their gallery just to build interest.

Retail Tips

Again, just like wholesaling, there are a ton of resources online about how to sell to a variety of different customer types in a retail environment, how to do fair booth or gallery setup and developing great customer service skills.

Here are a few tips I've learned over the years when selling in a retail environment:

- **Make Them Feel Special:** Remember, we've determined that people don't buy things they need, they buy things they want because of an emotional response. So when people approach you in a retail environment, whether it is an indoor show, outdoor fair or your own studio/gallery space, welcome them warmly and connect with them the way they want to connect. I call this mirroring. If someone is really friendly, then you be friendly. If someone is quiet, then you may want to be a little more subdued. If a customer is asking detailed questions, then talk shop and take them through your creative process. Understand? Just look them in the eye and connect.

- Be Interested, but Don't Pounce: Whatever you do, don't go into used car salesman mode, offering discounts, using pressure tactics or the like. People will let you know how much they want to engage. Be polite, friendly and be interested but don't tackle them while grabbing for their credit card.

- **Answer the Questions They are Asking:** This seems so basic but I need to say it. If someone is asking you about your creative process, then don't go into your pricing. Or, if a customer wants to know about care instructions for a potential purchase, don't start telling them about your college art school days. You can also anticipate other questions that the customer may not know to ask that are in line with their interests. Again, part of making a customer feel important is helping them get what they want.

- **Help Them Buy What They Want:** I have a variety of different lines in my work. You may as well. Each appeal to a different type of buyer. Some of my work is functional, some traditional, some contemporary and other sculptural. When a client shows interest in a certain style of your work, go with it. Don't try to force them into purchasing something they don't want just because you need to get rid of it. Give them ideas of how to use or display the piece in their home or office. Encourage them that their choice is a good one. Talk about what others have done who bought the same type of piece. Display the piece in ways that give clients ideas of how to use it once they get home.

- **Make It Easy to Do Business With You:** Do I even have to say this? You need to be taking credit cards. On your smartphone, you can use Square or PayPal very easily with no contract or large monthly fees.

You even get the card reader for free from Square. It just makes life so much easier. It's a no-brainer.

- **Stay Connected After the Sale:** Make sure you're encouraging your clients to follow your Facebook Business Page or Instagram account (we'll talk about that in a little while). Also, get their contact information so you can stay in touch through mail or email. This is invaluable information. It's easier to make a repeat sale than a first time sale. Remember, they already know and love you!

A Balanced Approach

There are some artists who only do wholesale, some only do retail and some do a combination of both. For me, I prefer a little of both for a few reasons. Wholesaling has a number of benefits including getting my work out there to a wider audience, providing regular orders (cash flow) throughout the year and being associated with fine retail establishments who increase my brand value in the eyes of the public. However, I don't overdo it. I really enjoy the connection with my customers, and to keep that in the mix, I do several retail shows a year, plus sell out of my own studio/gallery in Asheville, NC. I don't think I would ever go back to just doing one or the other. They both have their benefits. You just have to find out what works for you.

One of the best ways to find out about wholesaling is just to try it! Talk to other artists in your medium and ask for advice. Most are very willing to help you get started. A word about consignment – in general, I don't do it. If someone is not willing to purchase my product then they are less likely to work hard to sell it once it's on their shelf. That being said, I do have consignment work in a few galleries because of their reputation and I know that there, my work is going to sell. Play it by ear, but in my opinion, I wouldn't major on consignment. Even though you're getting your work out there, you're the one stuck waiting on your money.

Journaling Exercise

What are your thoughts about wholesale vs. retail? Are you interested in doing both? Just one? Explore your thoughts in your own journal and begin to develop a plan to focus your business.

Strategic Partnerships

Lastly in this chapter, I want to address the whole concept of strategic partnerships. Remember, you're not just an artist in the studio - you're a creative entrepreneur. That means you're always on the lookout for those who want to buy your product, sell your product, promote your product or get you in front of people who will.

When I say strategic partnership, don't let it freak you out. This is a really simple but powerful concept. It's basically making an intentional friendship with someone or some entity who is already in front of the people you want to be in front of, but who doesn't directly compete with you. This is very powerful because it becomes a mutually beneficial relationship. Let me give you an example.

My studio is in the River Arts District in Asheville, NC, and I'm the only professional basket maker in the city. However, many customers don't even know such an artist exists, much less come looking for me on their own. So, what do I do? I make friends! One of my best sales ever came from a pottery studio three doors down from me when a woman came in to purchase some pottery and began mentioning the fact that she would like to have some baskets as well. The potters immediately called me on my cell phone and told me to get down there quick! I brought about ten pieces with me from my gallery and the woman bought six at one time within about five minutes of me being there. Understand what I'm saying? Pottery has nothing to do with basketry but we are hitting the same type of clientele. We constantly refer each other, talk about each other's studio and encourage folks to visit after they finish with ours. When you have an attitude of abundance and joyful expectation, strategic partnerships become a powerful tool in your tool belt to grow your business.

Journaling Exercise

Who are some potential strategic partners that you could approach? What are some ways you could work together to enhance both your businesses?

Chapter 7

Getting Found Online:
Tools, Tips & Tricks for Online Marketing

Now it's time for some nuts and bolts details. I hope you're ready, because everything we've been talking about so far has been leading you to this point. You see, success in your art business is not about having big plans, lots of passion or even great art. Mind you, all those things are important but unless you have one thing, none of those others mean a hill of beans. What's the one thing you ask? Action. So buckle up, hold on and get ready for a big to-do list as you move through this chapter. Don't check out! I'll help you do this in manageable pieces so you can get the job done!

Let me set a foundation for our discussion regarding online marketing. These are some things that I don't want to assume, so pay attention and just like the GPS story at the beginning of the book, I'm asking you to recalculate your mind to a new reality. These five foundational pillars will be our focus during this chapter:

1. **Website**

   You must have a website. It's one of the first places people go to find your art. If you're not there, someone else will be.

2. **Quality Content**

   A bad website is worse than having no website at all. Old content, bad pictures or technical glitches only cause you to look like you don't know what you're doing. Just like when you do a show or walk into a gallery, you must put your best foot forward online and make sure your online presence represents who you really are.

3. **Search Engine Optimization**

   Just because you have a website doesn't mean anyone can find it. Unless you're working to make sure your website can be found, you might as well not have one.

4. **Link Popularity**

   Google likes you better when others like you first. Your website is not just a standalone entity, but rather it's a platform where you're connecting with your field, other artists, guilds, magazines, retailers and yes, potential and current customers.

5. **Social Media**

   Social Media is no longer an option. It's one of the best ways to connect with thousands of people all over the world for free and it can communicate the essence of your work and personality in ways that dry marketing fodder never could. However, to be successful it takes another reorientation of how you live as an artist. Don't worry, it's not that complicated and once you get started, it can be a lot of fun. We'll talk about social media in detail in the next chapter.

Ok, so now that you understand where we are going, let's dive right in!

Your Website

If you've made it this far, you're in one of two categories. You either have a website or you're about to get one! The point is, your website is your face to the world and in this new media world, it's non-negotiable. You must have one. So the question becomes not if you need one, but what kind to get, who's going to build and maintain it and what you need to do to get started.

I first started building websites back in the late 90's/early 2000's. Man, was it a different world – lots of complicated HTML code, expensive software and tons of headaches. Nowadays it's much more user-friendly, based on what we call a WYSIWYG system (what you see is what you get), and most everything you need lives in the cloud (or "on the internet" for you non-techie folks.)

There are lots of options out there for "do-it-yourself" websites including platforms like Weebly, Wix and Squarespace just to name a few. Here's what I like about these types of platforms:

- Very easy to use for novices or experts because of the versatile platform and tons of available themes that determine the style, color and layout of the website.

- You can do all the basics like add text, images, video, hyperlinks (links to other pages or files online), additional pages, forms and calendars while having some bells and whistles too like image sliders (rotating/clickable images), widgets (integrates other software into your website like email newsletters, gmail calendars, photo galleries, RSS news feeds and the like.)

- There's usually a free version or an upgraded version you can pay for.

- Lots of technical support and training available with each of these platforms and others like them. This makes your job a lot easier.

Quality Content

When you're building your website, remember, content is the most important aspect you should be considering.. Nobody wants to visit a website that has old, stale content. In order to keep your website fresh, you want to be updating the site regularly with fresh content. Examples of fresh content include things like images of recent work or you working in the studio, a blog article about your latest creative inspiration or a calendar update featuring your latest class. Also, if you get featured in a local magazine or newspaper, blog or website then link to that article. Post a video of you working on a project. Maybe do a short teaching video. The possibilities are really endless of what you could put on your website. The key is that you take the time to actually do the update (not just think about it) and that the content you're including is considered valuable to those interacting with your website. If you'll do that, then pretty soon, you'll start developing a solid reputation with followers and with the search engines.

Call to Action

One of the mistakes that artists make is thinking of their website as simply an online brochure. Sure, it can be that for you and I guess there's nothing really wrong with that other than you're cutting yourself short. Not only do you want people to visit your website, you want them to respond in some way; preferably the way you want them to respond. That response could be signing up for your e-newsletter, making a purchase, liking your Facebook page, following you on Instagram, sending you an email query about an upcoming class or downloading a free e-book you've written. We call this process a "call to action." In other words, you want to make it obvious and desirable for people to respond when they visit your website.

Lastly, you always want to give people the ability to easily share your website content with others via social media. There are tons of free plugins out there which allow you to embed sharing icons within your website.

Search Engine Optimization (SEO)

Ok, so there are tons of books that have been written on search engine optimization over the years. Everyone has their own mojo for it and I'm going to share mine with you. It's pretty simple. Since Google is the elephant in the room, I put most of my emphasis there.

Every page that goes on your website has a few components that you must learn to pay attention to and optimize for the most results. They include the Page Title, Page Description, Meta Tags, Keywords, Page Content, Image Titles and Image Descriptions. Each one of these components is like a bucket that holds information. What kind of information you ask? Primarily, they will hold what we call keywords or key phrases that clue the search engines, and ultimately potential site visitors, in on what your site is about. Let's take a minute to learn what each of these is for:

- **Page Title:** A very short, concise and compelling description of what's on the page. It's the most prominent thing people see when they search you on Google and it lives at the top of your webpage in the browser.

- **Page Description:** This is also a short, concise and compelling description of your webpage but this is what the search engine is going to display when it brings up the results of a search. It must go hand in hand with the Title.

- **Keywords:** A word or phrase used by search engines in their search for relevant web sites.

- **Page Content:** This is the text information on your website. This content is ultimately what's going to drive your page title, description and keywords. Unless your SEO optimization matches what the page is actually about, it's all for nothing.

- **Image Titles:** It's just like your page title except it's for an individual image. It's searchable once your image lives online and a major source of potential traffic for you when people are searching images on Google.

- **Image Descriptions (Alt Tags):** This is basically text that describes the image to people who are sight impaired. However, it also is used by Google to index images for searches, just like your normal webpage content. Don't forget them! When looking for art, many searchers will look through Google images first before the normal search listings because of the visual nature of the image listings. Good alt tags mean good rankings in Google images.

The great thing about keywords is that you don't have to make it a guessing game. Google provides a great free tool called the "Google Keyword Tool" where you can login to your Google account, put in possible search terms and the engine will generate a list of keywords and phrases that people are actually typing in when they go to Google looking for information. This is a very valuable tool, because it allows you to optimize the content of your website based on what keywords people are actually looking for.

It's also important to say at this point in our journey that over-optimization can really hurt you as well, so don't go overboard. What do I mean by overboard? The key to being successful in SEO is to diversify and make it natural. You can't just take all your keywords and pack them everywhere, in every page description, alt tag or page header. Rather, use them where they make sense naturally. Otherwise, you'll be seen by the search engine spiders as trying to game the system and you'll be penalized with lower page rankings, i.e. – you'll get buried.

Like I said, the key to successful optimization is natural diversification. Use a combination of three to four keywords or phrases in your page content (it has to make sense – don't just stick them in randomly), use one in your page title and your page heading, use a couple in your page description and then choose several to apply to your alt tags. Remember, your page description is what Google is going to display on the page ranking when someone searches and finds your website. Make sure it's accurate, clear and focused. For more on search engine optimization, check out Moz.com, KeywordTool.io or NeilPatel.com.

Link Popularity

One of the ways that search engines rank websites in their search results is by measuring how many other reputable sites within similar genres of information are linking back to a particular website. The more sites that do that, then the more valuable the search engines think the website is. Again, this needs to happen naturally, not in a spammy kind of way.

I would recommend a link building campaign that is based on your relationships. This would include reciprocal link sharing with other artist friends (you have their website listed on yours and vice versa), having a listing for your website on a guild, association or other industry leader website, having your website included on articles or blogs you write for other websites and having your website listed in various free and paid directories online.

You can build a link program into your website in two easy ways. First, you could easily have a list of artists or art organizations that you're affiliated with listed on your website; sort of a "friends of..." section. Remember, the point of this is that they link back to you as well! It's not enough for you just to have a link to them. That defeats the purpose. Secondly, if you're blogging, you could regularly feature other artists or affiliated art organizations that reciprocally link to you in a specific blog, thereby appearing more natural. Either way is a great option.

Social Media

Our whole next chapter is on social media. For this chapter, I simply want to encourage you to incorporate your social media activity into your website. Include your Facebook, Instagram, Twitter, Pinterest and other icons listed prominently on your website so people can click the icon and visit your site. Again, with most WYSIWYG-based website platforms, you can incorporate live feeds via widgets into your website so people can have real-time updates of your social media activity while browsing your site.

Lastly, don't forget about video, specifically YouTube! Creating a YouTube channel is easy, free and a must for everyone serious about search engine optimization for a number of reasons. First, video gives people a chance to connect with you in a very personal way that goes way beyond text and pictures on a page. Secondly, videos are very easy and popular to share on social media sites, blogs and other websites. Create a great video and it's likely to be shared within your genre by others who know and like you. That's huge! Lastly, YouTube is owned by Google, so everything you just learned about optimizing your website, keywords, descriptions and page titles works perfectly in YouTube. I've found over the years that YouTube videos I publish get to the top of the search engine rankings much, much quicker than normal pages. Again, it's not a magic bullet, but it's another great tool in your SEO tool-belt.

Journaling Exercise

When it comes to your online marketing, there are a lot of details to juggle. Let's take just a moment and get organized, ok?

Do you have a website yet? If not, what do you need to do to make that happen? By when? How much do you need to invest? What do you want your website to do for you? (Is it a brochure, an online sales platform, a gallery?) Make a list of goals for your website with a timeframe for completion.

Take a moment right now and go search using one of the tools I mentioned.. Then, follow the directions and begin a search for your most appropriate key words and phrases. Once you have a strong list of 10-20, then record them somewhere for future use in your website, articles, image tagging, social media and press releases. You can record them here for nowUsing your list of strategic partners that you developed a few chapters back and contact them about doing a 'link sharing' campaign with you online. This could include both your website and also social-media outlets.

Chapter 8

Staying Connected: How to Leverage Social Media

I've been engaged in marketing for about 20+ years now professionally, both in the nonprofit sector and various b2b (business to business) and b2c (business to consumer) markets. During that time, my core marketing values have always gone back to one basic principle – strategic partnerships. I learned early on that it's a lot easier to develop friendships and sell with people than to see everyone out there as potential competition. Ultimately, this comes from my foundational belief in the laws of abundance and attraction that we discussed in the first chapter of this book; the more I help others get what they want, the more I receive what I want and need.

This understanding is core to being successful at social media because if you don't come at it from this perspective, social media can seem on the surface like a colossal waste of time. However, it's my belief that social media is one of the most powerful tools we've ever been given as artists and as entrepreneurs to connect with potential clients and strategic partners in a natural, relational way that promotes interaction.

Social Media is about Relationships

I'll be the first to admit it. It's very easy for me to put my marketing hat on and see social media interaction as just another tool to be used to get sales. That's a mistake. If you ever lose sight of social media's real power, it will lose its value and impact in your business. At the end of the day, social media is about the development and growth of relationships, not just about numbers. It's like everything in life. If you go after the numbers and the money, they will always elude you. However, if you pursue your passion with excellence while developing real, authentic relationships the money will always follow. Social media is the same way. You've got to focus on the relationship and interaction with people and let it develop over time. It's a long-term investment that can yield powerful, potentially profitable results.

Like everything in our oversaturated, media mash world, it can be confusing to know what social media outlets to avoid and which ones to pursue with vigor. None of us have unlimited time and resources to just sit around all day on the computer posting and tweeting away the day. So, I'd like to make five recommendations for your social media portfolio: Facebook, Instagram, Pinterest, LinkedIn and YouTube. Of the five, my favorite and what I find the easiest to use is Facebook, but we'll cover all of them.

I can't possibly give you every detail of all five of these social media platforms in this short book. However, I'd like to give you some of my best practices regarding each of them in order to be signposts for success.

Facebook

I've been on Facebook since it came out and have been a huge fan ever since. Yes, it's had its ups and downs like every tech platform out there, but for the time and energy I invest in it each day, I find it's where I get the most bang for my buck.

So what's so great about Facebook? For the artist, I think it's two-fold: interaction and images. Facebook makes it so easy to connect with people and have conversations around what they feel is important through both personal interactions with "friends" and conversations with people in "groups" and on pages you "like." It also gives you a huge platform to be able to display, share and house all the images and videos you want to promote. I'm always amazed at who shares my images online and how far the reach goes! Lastly, they have incredible measurement tools available for users to allow you to see how many people you're reaching each week via each post. This is invaluable for entrepreneurs because it allows you to see what people in the market are responding to so you can respond in turn.

I get asked a lot by artists, "Should I have a personal account or business account on Facebook?" The answer is both. You need that personal connection with people to build relationships while also promoting your art business through interactions on a fan page, as well.

Like all social media, you should post at least daily with good quality content worth reading or seeing. This is literally as easy as sharing a good article you've just read, a new snapshot of a piece you're working on in the studio or just a pithy comment. This is especially easy to do now via the apps on your smartphone. Please don't be one of those annoying people who use social media as a political soapbox. Nobody likes it, it's annoying and your social media capital goes way down when people start blocking your posts.

Tips for Facebook:

- Be a good friend. "Friend" others liberally, "like" other pages that represent your values, "comment" on and "share" things that you're interested in and stuff that your friends are doing. It all goes together to make sure people know you're in the game and interested in what they are doing.

- When you start your own personal profile and fan page, make sure you keep it "public" and allow people to comment and post on your page. Remember, Facebook is all about interaction, not just you pushing your ideas.

- Join "groups" that are in your same genre to widen your interactions with others who are interested in the same things. If there isn't one out there you like, then start and promote your own group. That will help to establish you as an expert online.

- Change your profile and timeline cover photos often, just keep it fresh.

- Use event pages to promote openings, classes, sales or other events you're promoting online.

- Consider purchasing ads or promoting your posts when appropriate. It's typically a small investment that puts your content in front of a much wider audience.

- When starting your "business page", make sure to incorporate your business name into the title. If that's not available then try to use a great keyword or phrase that will help boost your SEO.

- Personally thank new friends and followers when they connect with you.

- Complete your profile section and make sure to add your website address.

Instagram

Instagram is not Facebook so think about them differently. Instagram is a much more image and video focused platform. Just like Facebook, you have a choice to have a personal or a business account. Again, I'd recommend you have both and use this platform to promote who you are both personally and professionally, unless you just don't have the time to do both.

Tips for Instagram

- Choose a great profile image that represents what you do creatively. Use an image of your work or you in the studio. If you have a logo, consider using that as well.

- Use #hashtags in order to connect with others who are talking about the same topics on Instagram.

- Use LinkTree to share multiple links to your website, classes and products.

- Don't be boring. Again, share valuable content that reflects your interests, expertise and most of all, your creative voice. Be bold.

- Comment on posts that you like often and thank those who comment on your posts. It's all about building the network and that's all about real relationships.

- Explore all the capabilities Instagram has to offer like Reels, IGTV, Stories and of course normal image and video posts.

- Find people, groups or organizations to follow and connect with them. Also, thank your new followers via a short personal message.

- Complete your profile section and make sure to add your website address. This is a great place for incorporating a strategic keyphrase to help people find you as they search.

Pinterest

I love Pinterest for a few reasons. First of all, it's just eye-candy for the creative mind! I love that I can go on there and be inspired by other peoples' creativity in one place. Secondly, I love the fact that I can use Pinterest as my own creative treasure trove of inspiration by creating boards that inspire me. I have specific boards for specific interests. I used to do this through "bookmarks" in my browser. Pinterest makes it so much easier now to have all those great images in one place. Lastly, I love it when my work gets shared and goes viral. It's just helping to build my artistic brand.

Just a note of caution – there's a lot of controversy about Pinterest among artists, especially photographers, who feel kind of ripped off by the whole platform. I get that, but I also understand that there's not a downside when my work is being shared. So, if you're concerned about that either don't use the platform, or watermark your images with your name, website or logo so people know it's yours.

Tips for Pinterest

- Consider logging to your account via Facebook and connect the accounts. It allows you to connect your social media worlds and ultimately pick up more followers, friends and pins. Plus it's easy. You can also connect your Instagram account as well.

- Upload all your own work on a board, making it easy for others to share. Be sure to include a nice description, copyright and website link in the description of each image.

- Re-Pin other images you like on your boards. Follow other boards that you connect with. Again, it just keeps you in the game, building relationships.

- Pinterest is almost 70% women, most of whom are mothers, so remember to be interesting to those who are following you.

LinkedIn

From a professional perspective, there's no larger networking platform out there than LinkedIn. The key word here on LinkedIn is "professional". This platform is not Facebook or Instagram, in that it's really not the place for quick snapshots of your work, pithy sayings or other casual conversation. It's about promoting yourself as a professional artist.

Tips for LinkedIn:

- Connect with business friends like suppliers, gallery owners and current/potential clients.

- Create a great profile that lets people know who you are and what you've done. Include a link to your website and other social media platforms.

- Use an artist shot of you working for your profile picture, not just a boring business headshot.

- Join a group. There are tons of groups on LinkedIn that promote conversation and connection.

- Be careful about connecting your social media accounts with LinkedIn. If you do, remember the nature of this platform is more professional and so your posts or tweets need to reflect that.

- Recommend others that you're connected with and request that others do the same. It's kind of like "following" on Instagram or "liking" on Facebook.

YouTube

Ok, so I love me some YouTube! Why? Because video connects you to people in a way that normal text and pictures never can. There's a personal connection that happens when people see you speak, move and create that can't be matched anywhere else other than real, in-person interactions. I also love YouTube because it is owned by Google, and that means that Google is paying attention to what's on there. Once you learn to optimize your channel and videos, you have an incredible opportunity to connect with tons of people online.

Tips for YouTube

- Use video to tell your story. Bring people into your everyday creative activities and let them see what's really going on with you. I have a friend who's a potter and sometimes he'll just set his phone up in front of him while he's throwing pots and let the video go for about three minutes while he's working... he rarely says anything but it's really cool to watch his process.

- Optimize your videos when you are uploading to YouTube just like you would a normal web page, based on what I taught you earlier about keywords, titles, tags, etc.

- Embed your videos into your website. YouTube gives you the ability to embed your videos by providing you with the HTML embed code. Just copy it and paste it into the HTML part of your web page and boom, you have video on your website.

- Share your videos via social media. Again, YouTube gives you the ability to share the link via Facebook,

Instagram and other social media outlets. It's a great way to drive traffic to your channel and build buzz on social media sites.

- Consider doing tutorial or "ask the expert" videos. The more videos you do like this, where you are showing people how to do a certain technique or process, the more you'll be seen as an expert in what you're doing. You can then share those videos on your website, on social media and within groups and other blogs that are in your genre. Hopefully, others will pick it up, share and endorse, ultimately driving more traffic.

- Keep it simple and short. You don't have to produce professionally shot videos that are thirty minutes in length to be successful on YouTube. That's part of the charm of the platform. Literally shooting with your iPhone camera, dropping it in iMovie or another simple editing platform, doing some simple editing and uploading via the internet is all you have to do. Don't over think it.

Journaling Exercise

Take just a moment and in your own journal, write down the things you're doing currently with social media. What's working and what's not? What would you like to pursue in the coming months?

Chapter 9

Plan to Succeed: The 90-Day Challenge

The old adage says, "Fail to Plan and Plan to Fail." I couldn't agree more. There would be nothing worse for me, as one who loves to help creative people thrive in their gifting, than to hear that you read this book and then failed to implement anything. You may think, "Oh, I would never do that!" But that's exactly what most folks do. They read a book, highlight a few things, continually say, "oh, I know that…" and keep going with business as usual. I hope that's not you, my friend!

Over the years, I've realized that people do what they want to do. I know that sounds simplistic, but at the end of the day it's a universal truth. If you want to do something bad enough, then you'll find a way no matter the cost. So knowing that, this is the place in the book where I get to ask you the one million dollar question – what do you really want? Because unless you clarify that and begin to make some movement toward that goal with specific steps, you're going to look back in six months, a year, even ten years and think "Why haven't things changed?" The reason will be not because the world was against you, or you weren't as talented as the artist in the next studio, or even because that other artist knew the magazine editor of the publication that was supposed to feature you, but rather, the cause for little or no progress will be because you chose not to act.

Journaling Exercise

Take a moment in your own journal and clarify what it is that you want; big picture with no limits, for your art business and for yourself personally. Write it down as it flows from your heart and don't judge it. Just let it come out.

Now that you're beginning to get some clarity around what you want, I'm going to encourage you to go through a process that I started doing several years back. This process not only changed my life, but it has become a regular part of how I live and lead. It's called 90-Day planning.

You see, there's no possible way that you can take everything in this book and implement it all at one time. You'd be busier than a one-legged man in a butt kicking contest, have zero creative energy left and be totally overwhelmed. However, you can learn to prioritize and plan your life – both personally and in business – so that you're moving toward the goals you have in mind for yourself.

SMARTi Goals

Before we talk about the exact goals you want to set for yourself, it's important to understand what type of goals are the most helpful. Most of us would say things like, "I want to be a better dad," or "I want to be successful," or "I want to sell more of my art next year." All of them are great aspirations, but the problem is you never know when you've achieved them. They are just broad-based wishes with no teeth. Rather, I want to encourage you to set SMARTi[3] goals. That is, goals that are Specific, Measurable, Attainable, Relevant and that have a Timeframe with an Incentive.

- **Specific:** Instead of saying something like, "I want to be a better dad to my son." a specific goal would be, "to spend three hours every Saturday morning hanging out with my son at home." Does that make sense? It is defined, not just generalized.

- **Measurable:** A measurable goal means that it has some sort of standard by which you can determine whether or not you've done it. For example, instead of saying, "I want to get my work into some more galleries this year," a measurable goal would be, "to have my artwork accepted into three new galleries by September 30, 2013." There is a number of galleries

---

[3] *The original SMART goals were developed by George Doran, Arthur Miller and James Cunningham in their 1981 article "There's a S.M.A.R.T. way to write management goals and objectives"*

and a timeframe specified that you can use to measure your success.

- **Attainable:** When you are setting a goal, don't set something out there that you absolutely know you will not be able to attain. For example, if you're selling five pieces of your art a month, don't set a goal your first month to sell thirty pieces by the end of next month. Barring an absolute miracle, it's not going to happen. Be realistic that the goals you're setting are stretching you but at the same time are within your skill, ability and bandwidth.

- **Relevant:** Believe it or not, it's important to set goals that actually have something to do with your overall life and career goals. Many times people have aspirations to do things that have nothing to do with moving them closer to their ultimate goals. Remember, your ability to say no to the wrong things allows you the freedom to say yes to the right things.

- **Timeframe:** Again, it's important to give yourself a defined deadline to achieve your goals. "One day" will never come, but Tuesday, February 5 at 5pm is a real time that you can measure your success by. Plus, a deadline puts a little fire under your seat.

- **Incentive:** We all like rewards. When you're crafting your SMARTi goals, give yourself an incentive to achieve, like a special dinner out with your significant other, a new tool you've been wanting or a vacation. It can be as simple or as extravagant as you want. Just do something to reward your effort and achievement.

Personal Goals

Let's start with some personal goals because I'm one of those people who believes that unless your personal life is flowing, your creative and business life are never going to flourish. This is not about choosing one part of our life over another, but rather learning to thrive as creative people in the midst of everything we have to do and get to do.

What are three personal goals you have for the next 90 days? List them below, writing the goal itself in "Goal", the deadline in "Timeframe" and who's responsible in "Responsible." Most of the time that is you, but in a team environment, this is very helpful for everyone to see what each other is doing.

Business Goals

Now that you have some personal goals that you're working toward, let's set some for your business. I'd encourage you right now to go back through the chapters and journaling exercises in this book and pull out some of the highlights that you really want to focus on over the next 90 days. Then turn them into SMARTi goals and list them below. Feel free to add as many as you like. These could include things like developing a marketing plan, following up with some strategic partners, forming a corporation or even pursuing some new wholesale opportunities.

Creative Goals

Lastly, I'd like for you to think in terms of setting some creative goals. These are goals that directly affect your creativity and art process. They could be things like learning a new technique, taking a class, setting aside time each week for an artist date to feed your creative side or exploring a new medium. At the end of these first 90 days, you'll be amazed at how much you've accomplished and how excited you are to keep moving forward. If you miss one of your goals, don't sweat it – just adjust and keep moving. I'd recommend doing this as an ongoing discipline in your creative life, as you continue to craft your brand.

Lastly, I'd love to hear your feedback on how this book has helped you. And, if you're ready to take the next step of becoming a part of my Created to Thrive Artist Mentoring Program, then be sure to visit me at www.MattTommeyMentoring.com for all the information. Also, please connect with me on social media

@thethrivingchristianartist and on my podcast, The Thriving Christian Artist.

It's really been my pleasure to walk you through this journey. Now it's up to you! Go for it!

About the Author

Matt is a woven sculpture artist from Asheville, North Carolina, and an internationally known Christian speaker, author of several books. He is also a mentor to artists from around the world through his "Created to Thrive" Artist Mentoring Program and The Thriving Christian Artist podcast.

In 2009, God called Matt to "raise up an army of artists to reveal His glory all over the earth." Since then, Matt has given his life to helping artists thrive spiritually, creatively, and in business through creating live events, resources, and online opportunities that equip artists to live the life they were divinely designed to live in the Kingdom.

As an artist, Matt's work has been featured in many magazines, shows, and exhibitions and is mostly commissioned by private clients for luxury mountain and coastal homes around the country. In 2011, Matt was recognized by the Smithsonian American Art Museum's Renwick Gallery as an American Artist Under 40. In 2018, Matt was recognized as one of the Best Artist Mentors in the country by Professional Artist Magazine.

Other Resources from Matt Tommey

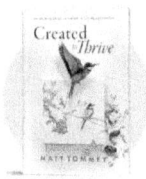

Books by Matt Tommey

To see Matt's full line of books, visit MattTommeyMentoring.com/resources

The Thriving Christian Artist Podcast

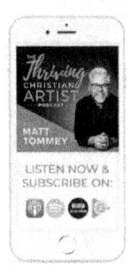

Matt's twice weekly podcast can be found at MattTommeyMentoring.com/podcast

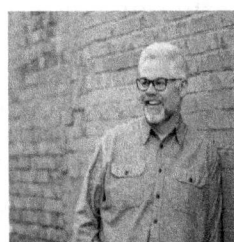

Matt's Blog

If you love the podcast, then check out Matt's weekly blog that picks up where the podcast ends found at MattTommeyMentoring.com/blog

The Artist Mentoring Program

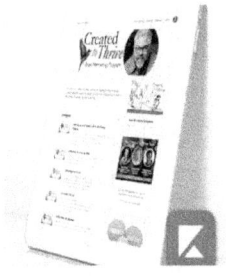

An easy-to-follow, online mentorship program, dedicated to helping Christian artists become confident and equipped in their creative callings. To learn more, visit MattTommeyMentoring.com/artmentor

www.ingramcontent.com/pod-product-compliance
Lightning Source LLC
Chambersburg PA
CBHW071722170526
45165CB00005B/2122